MARY M. COVEY

Celebrations!

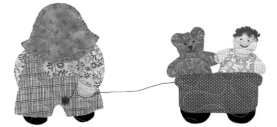

Quilts for
Cherished Family Moments

Martingale™
& COMPANY

Martingale™
& COMPANY

That Patchwork Place®

That Patchwork Place® is an imprint of Martingale & Company™.

Celebrations! Quilts for Cherished Family Moments
© 2002 by Mary M. Covey

Martingale & Company
20205 144th Avenue NE
Woodinville, WA 98072-8478 USA
www.martingale-pub.com

Printed in Hong Kong
07 06 05 04 03 02   8 7 6 5 4 3 2 1

CREDITS

President	Nancy J. Martin
CEO	Daniel J. Martin
Publisher	Jane Hamada
Editorial Director	Mary V. Green
Managing Editor	Tina Cook
Technical Editor	Laurie Baker
Copy Editor	Melissa Bryan
Design Director	Stan Green
Illustrator	Laurel Strand
Cover and Text Designer	Trina Stahl
Photographer	Brent Kane

Library of Congress Cataloging-in-Publication Data

Covey, Mary M.
   Celebrations! : quilts for cherished family moments / Mary M. Covey.
      p. cm.
   ISBN 1-56477-445-7
  1. Quilting—Patterns. 2. Appliqué—Patterns. I. Title.
   TT835 .C6937 2002
   746.46'041—dc21

MISSION STATEMENT

*We are dedicated to providing quality products
and service by working together to inspire creativity
and to enrich the lives we touch.*

Dedication

To Kaisha Gabriel, for her continuous encouragement and unwavering friendship.

Acknowledgments

My sincere gratitude and appreciation go to:
Shirley Covey, my sister-in-law, for helping with buttonhole stitching,
cutting triangles, and stitching bindings. Her help was priceless.
The staff at Martingale & Company, especially Dawn Anderson and Terry Martin,
for always being enthusiastic, encouraging, and patient.
I am more grateful than words can say.
Laurie Baker for her editing expertise. Thanks, Laurie!

Contents

Introduction

WHEN SOMETHING SPECIAL happens in my immediate or extended family, we have a celebration. No matter what the event, whether it is the birth of a new baby, moving into a new home, or sending a child off to college, family and friends are brought together to celebrate. And with them come their culinary specialties—fried chicken, mashed potatoes, casseroles, pies, cakes, etc. If I were a great cook like my mother, who could make the best chocolate cake without even using a recipe, I would bake something for these special events. But, I am a quilter. Therefore, each of these events becomes an inspiration for a new quilt.

Just like a cook, I start by searching out just the right recipe, or in this case the right design, for the event. Then I gather my ingredients—the fabrics, threads, and embellishments—and mix them into a variety of blocks, sashings, and borders, until I achieve the perfect combination.

The memory of how wonderful my mother's chocolate cake tasted has faded, but not the memory of the love that went into each cake. Making a quilt to celebrate life's events gives the one who receives the quilt a tangible memento of the event that can be shared with family and friends and then passed on. The one who gives knows the joy that comes from creating a lasting memory.

Whether you have a family that celebrates any and every event, or a family that celebrates only traditional events, I hope you find pleasure in making the projects in this book. You might be amazed and delighted to discover the memories that can be sewn into a quilt. Celebrate the joy of creating!

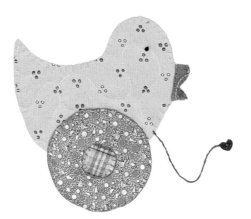

General Directions

In this section we'll cover the basics—fabric, tools, cutting methods, piecing techniques—and the different ways you can embellish your quilts with embroidery stitches.

Fabric Selection

Fabric, fabric everywhere, but which ones do you choose? Without a doubt, fabric is the most important ingredient in the quilting recipe, but with so many choices, selecting just the right combination can be overwhelming. Here are a few guidelines to help you through the process.

Content, Color, and Care

There are lots of fabric choices available, but nothing works better for quilting than 100 percent–cotton fabrics. They hold their shape well and are easy to handle. The variety of 100 percent–cotton fabrics to choose from is unbelievable—solids, prints, plaids, stripes, brushed cotton, flannels, and so on. These fabrics are available from your local quilt shop, by mail order, and even online!

When selecting fabrics, use a variety of designs, textures, colors, and styles. To enhance the main fabric colors, avoid using solid white or off-white for your background fabric. Instead, opt for tone-on-tone or white-on-white prints to add dimension to your project. And while it's easy to get caught up in all the luscious fabrics, always work with colors that you like. The colors of the fabrics you choose are what will make the quilt truly your own. Trust your instincts to guide you.

Yardage requirements are provided for all of the projects in this book and are based on 42" of usable fabric after preshrinking. Some quilts call for an assortment of scraps. If you have your own scraps or have access to someone else's scraps, these quilts provide a great opportunity to use them. If you are a new quilter and haven't built up your scrap collection yet, or if you just want to add to your collection, purchase an assortment of fat quarters to give your quilt the same "scrappy" feel.

Before using your fabrics, wash them in warm water, using mild laundry soap with no bleach additives or a soap that is made specifically for washing quilts. Make sure to wash dark and light colors separately so that the dyes from the dark colors will not run onto light fabrics. Some fabrics may require several rinses to eliminate the excess dyes. Dry the fabrics in the dryer; then press them so you can accurately cut out the pieces for the quilt.

Grain Lines

The characteristics of the lengthwise, crosswise, and bias grains are important to know so that you can work with them and not against them to achieve the best finished product. The lengthwise grain line runs parallel to the selvage edges of the fabric and has very little stretch. The crosswise grain line runs from selvage to selvage and has some give to it. Cutting on either the lengthwise or crosswise grain is considered "cutting on grain." The true bias grain line runs at a 45° angle to the lengthwise and cross-wise grain lines and has a substantial amount of give when pulled. Edges cut on the bias should be handled carefully, as they easily can stretch out of shape.

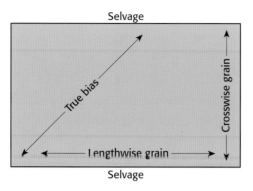

When rotary cutting fabric, start by cutting strips of fabric along the crosswise grain, unless otherwise indicated. Cut shapes, such as squares and rectangles, from the strips along the lengthwise grain. That way when you sew the pieces back together, the threads will lie naturally, as the fabric was originally woven. This will prevent stretching and buckling in a quilt top. In appliqué, as long as the background is cut on the lengthwise or crosswise grain, the pieces being appliquéd will not become distorted.

Tools and Supplies

GOOD TOOLS are essential for any job that needs to be done right, and quilting is no exception. You probably own most of the general sewing tools and supplies needed for quilting, but read through the following sections just to be sure. If you need to purchase any new equipment, invest in the best quality that you can afford. It is much more enjoyable to piece and quilt your projects when you use equipment and supplies that consistently produce good results. Most of these items are available at quilt shops or fabric shops.

EMBROIDERY FLOSS OR PEARL COTTON

For the four quilts in this book that are accented with appliqué motifs, you will need to add decorative stitching, using either embroidery floss or #8 pearl cotton.

IRON AND IRONING BOARD

Careful pressing is a must if you want to achieve accurate piecing. Keep your iron and ironing board as close to your sewing area as possible. You may spray fabrics with water or spray sizing when pressing, but it is best not to use the steam feature on your iron if it has one. The force and temperature at which the steam is emitted from the iron can stretch fabric and make it difficult to work with.

NEEDLES

For machine piecing, start each project with a new, sharp sewing-machine needle in a size 10/70 or 12/80. A dull needle can distort seams, snag fabric, and cause skipped stitches. For hand piecing and appliqué, use size 11 or size 12 Sharps, which are thinner than other sewing needles. For hand quilting, use size 8, 9, or 10 Betweens. Betweens are shorter and thinner than regular sewing needles, allowing you to work through the layers of a quilt more easily and make smaller stitches. To make the embroidery stitches on the appliqué quilts, use a size 8 embroidery needle.

PAPER-BACKED FUSIBLE TRANSFER WEB

Several of the quilts in this book include appliquéd motifs that are applied to the project with fusible web. There are many paper-backed transfer webs on the market; choose one that is lightweight and can

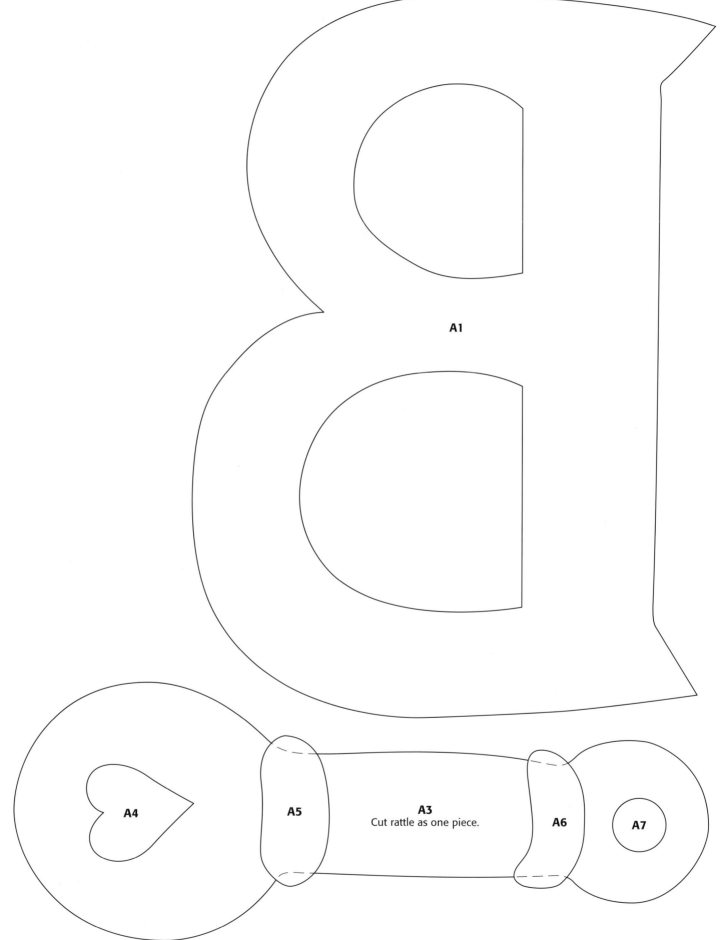

A1

A4

A5

A3
Cut rattle as one piece.

A6

A7

the color placement of the blocks so matching blocks will be in opposing corners when the quilt is completed.

2. Layer the quilt top with batting and backing; baste.

3. Quilt as desired.

4. Bind the quilt edges with the print binding strips.

5. Stitch a label to the quilt back.

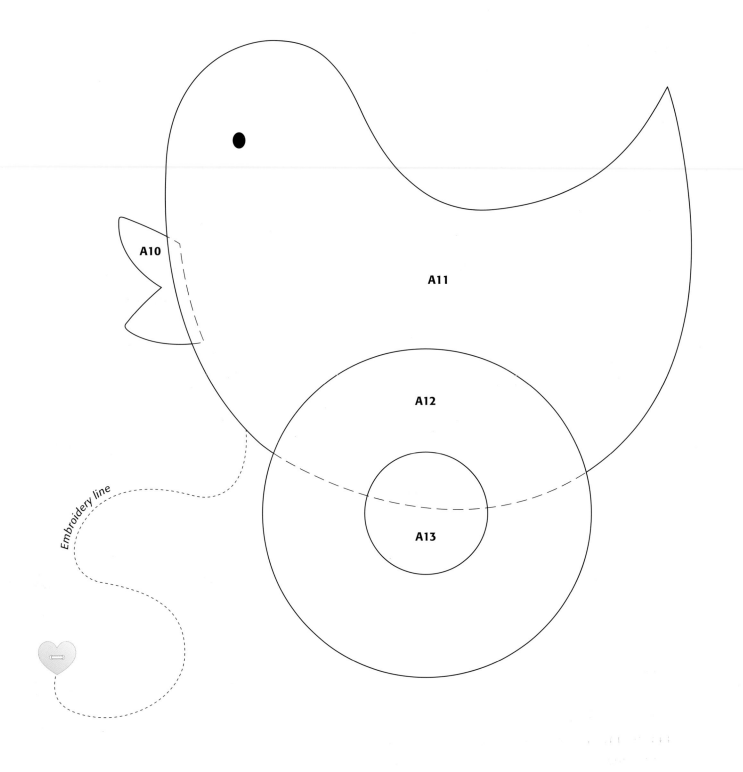

A10

A11

A12

A13

Embroidery line

Quilt-Top Assembly

1. Refer to "Fusible-Web Appliqué" on page 14 to prepare and cut the appliqués from the remaining fat-quarter fabrics, using patterns A1–A14 on pages 31–34. Trace and cut out 2 *each* of A1 and A9, 4 of A2, and 1 *each* of the remaining motifs. Fuse the pieces to the 9½" x 9½" white-on-white squares, using the project photo and the appliqué patterns as placement guides.

2. After all of the appliqués have been fused in place, refer to "Embroidery Stitches" on page 15 to outline each shape with a buttonhole stitch, or use the buttonhole stitch option on your sewing machine and machine stitch around each shape. Refer to the pattern to mark the pull string for the duck toy on the appliqué square. Stemstitch the pull string and satin stitch the heart at the end of the string. Use the marker to make the duck's eye.

3. To make the Nine Patch blocks, stitch 5 identical print and 4 white-on-white 3½" x 3½" squares together into 3 horizontal rows as shown. Press the seams toward the print squares. Stitch the rows together. Press the seams in one direction. Make 8 for the quilt top. Repeat with the print and white 2½" x 2½" squares to make 4 Nine Patch blocks for the border corners.

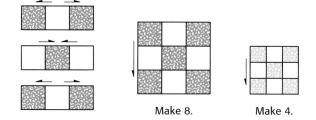

Make 8.   Make 4.

4. Stitch the appliqué and quilt-top Nine Patch blocks into 4 horizontal rows of 2 appliqué blocks and 2 Nine Patch blocks each, arranging the blocks in each row as shown. Press the seams toward the appliqué blocks. Stitch the rows together. Press the seams in one direction.

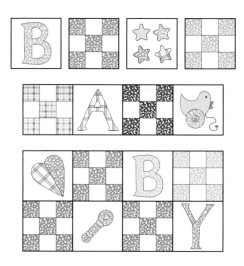

Quilt Finishing

REFER TO "Finishing Your Quilt" on pages 17–25.

1. Referring to "Borders with Corner Squares" on page 19, cut the borders to the appropriate size. Stitch the side borders to the quilt-top sides. Stitch a border-corner Nine Patch block from step 3 in "Quilt-Top Assembly" to each end of the 2 remaining border strips. Alternate

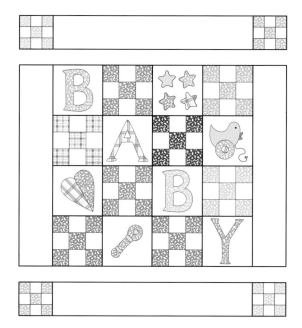

What new mother wouldn't love to wrap her bundle of joy in this sweet quilt? Appliquéd with baby motifs suitable for a boy or a girl, it would be lovely as a wall hanging, too. The quilt is finished with stipple quilting, which is perfect for projects that will receive lots of love and laundry time.

Nine Patch Block
Finished size: 9"

Nine Patch Block
Finished size: 6"

Appliqué Block
Finished size: 9"

Materials

Yardage is based on 42"-wide fabric.

- 1 fat quarter each of 12 assorted prints for Nine Patch blocks and appliqués
- 1⅞ yds. white-on-white print for Nine Patch blocks, appliqué blocks, and border
- 3 yds. fabric for backing
- ½ yd. print for binding
- 56" x 56" square of batting
- ¾ yd. paper-backed fusible transfer web
- Embroidery floss to match appliqués
- Fine-tip black permanent marker

Cutting

All measurements include ¼"-wide seam allowances.

From the white-on-white print, cut:

- 2 strips, 9½" x 42". Crosscut the strips into 8 squares, 9½" x 9½", for appliqué blocks.
- 3 strips, 3½" x 42". Crosscut the strips into 32 squares, 3½" x 3½", for quilt-top Nine Patch blocks.
- 1 strip, 2½" x 42". Crosscut the strip into 16 squares, 2½" x 2½", for border-corner Nine Patch blocks.
- 4 strips, 6½" x 42", for borders

From *each* of 8 fat-quarter prints, cut:

- 1 strip (8 total), 3½" x 18". Crosscut *each* strip into 5 squares (40 total), 3½" x 3½", for quilt-top Nine Patch blocks.

From *each* of 2 of the remaining fat-quarter prints, cut:

- 2 strips (4 total), 2½" x 18". Crosscut *each pair of strips* into 10 squares (20 total), 2½" x 2½", for border corner Nine Patch blocks.

From the binding fabric, cut:

- 5 strips, 2½" x 42"

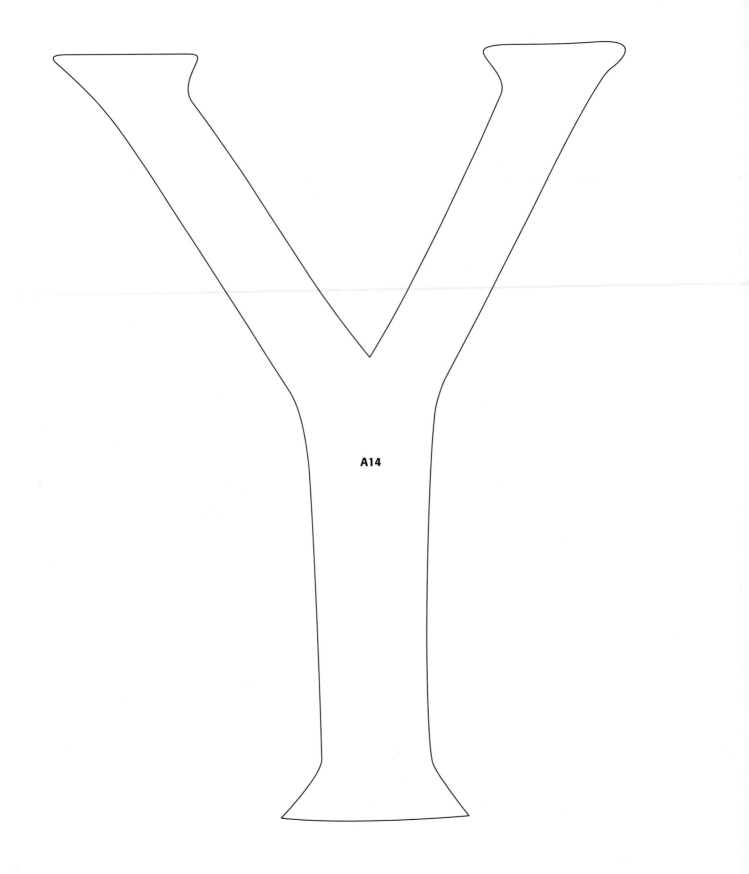

A14

A "big kid" bed deserves a big kid quilt. This quilt is just the right size for a toddler bed, but you can adjust it to fit a twin-size bed by adding an extra row of blocks to the bottom and one side and adjusting the borders.

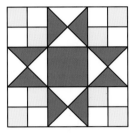

Star Block
Finished size: 15"

Materials

Yardage is based on 42"-wide fabric.

- 2⅛ yds. blue for blocks, inner border, outer border, and binding
- 2⅛ yds. white for blocks and sashing
- 1 yd. yellow for blocks, sashing corner posts, and middle border
- Assorted fabric scraps for appliqués
- 3¾ yds. fabric for backing
- 60" x 79" rectangle of batting
- ½ yd. paper-backed fusible web
- Embroidery floss to match appliqués and for doll hair and kite strings
- ¼"-diameter button for end of wagon pull string
- ½ yd. of ¼"-wide ribbon for kite tail ballasts
- Fine-tip black and red permanent markers

Cutting

All measurements include ¼"-wide seam allowances.

From the blue fabric, cut:
- 1 strip, 5½" x 42". Crosscut the strip into 6 squares, 5½" x 5½", for block centers.
- 2 strips, 6½" x 42". Crosscut the strips into 12 squares, 6½" x 6½", for block quarter-square-triangle units.
- 6 strips, 1½" x 42", for inner border
- 6 strips, 3½" x 42", for outer border
- 7 strips, 2½" x 42", for binding

From the white fabric, cut:
- 2 strips, 6½" x 42". Crosscut the strips into 12 squares, 6½" x 6½", for block quarter-square-triangle units.
- 4 strips, 3" x 42", for block four-patch units
- 9 strips, 4½" x 42". Crosscut the strips into 17 rectangles, 4½" x 15½", for sashing.

From the yellow fabric, cut:
- 4 strips, 3" x 42", for block four-patch units
- 2 strips, 4½" x 42". Crosscut the strips into 12 squares, 4½" x 4½", for sashing corner posts.
- 6 strips, 1½" x 42", for middle border

I'm a Big Kid Now

Finsihed quilt size: 52" x 71"

6. To make the block rows, alternately stitch together 3 white 4½" x 15½" sashing strips and 2 Star blocks, beginning and ending with a sashing strip. Make 3 block rows.

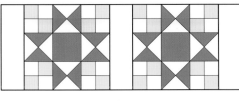

Make 3.

7. To make the sashing rows, alternately stitch together 3 yellow 4½" x 4½" squares and 2 white 4½" x 15½" sashing strips, beginning and ending with a yellow square. Make 4 sashing rows.

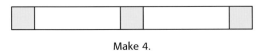

Make 4.

8. Beginning and ending with a sashing row, alternately stitch together the 4 sashing and 3 block rows.

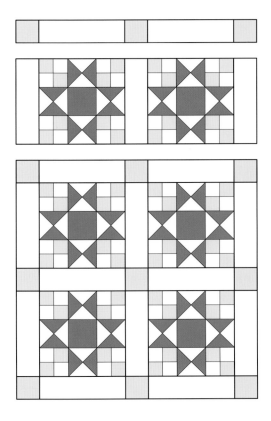

Quilt Finishing

REFER TO "Finishing Your Quilt" on pages 17–25.

1. Referring to "Borders with Mitered Corners" on page 18, stitch the blue and yellow 1½" x 42" strips and the blue 3½" x 42" strips together as shown to make one long border unit. Measure and cut the border strips as instructed and stitch them to the quilt top, placing the blue inner-border strip closest to the quilt top.

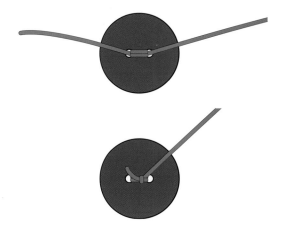

2. Refer to "Fusible-Web Appliqué" on page 14 to prepare and cut the appliqués from the assorted fabric scraps, using patterns B1–B21 on pages 40–41. Trace and cut out 2 of B18 and 1 *each* of the remaining motifs. Fuse the pieces to the quilt top, using the project photo and the appliqué patterns as placement guides.

3. After all of the appliqués have been fused in place, refer to "Embroidery Stitches" on page 15 to outline each shape with a buttonhole stitch, or use the buttonhole stitch option on your sewing machine and machine stitch around each shape. Refer to the photo as a guide for marking the curly line that connects

Quilt-Top Assembly

1. Draw 2 diagonal lines on the wrong side of each white 6½" x 6½" square as shown. Lay each marked white square on top of a blue 6½" x 6½" square, right sides together. Stitch ¼" away from each side of one line. Cutting on the unsewn line first, cut each square into quarters along the drawn lines. Press the seam allowances toward the blue fabric to make pieced triangles. Make 48.

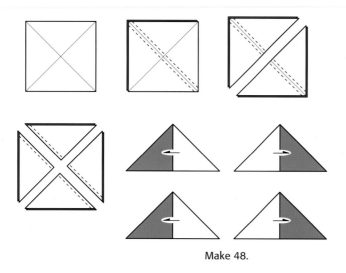

Make 48.

2. Stitch 2 pieced triangles together as shown to make a quarter-square-triangle unit. Press the seam in one direction. Trim the unit to 5½" x 5½". Make 24.

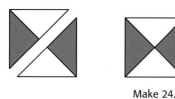

Make 24.

3. Referring to "Making Strip Sets" on page 13, stitch a white 3" x 42" strip to a yellow 3" x 42" strip. Press the seam allowance toward the yellow fabric. Make 4. Cut the strip sets into 48 segments, 3" wide.

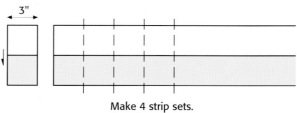

Make 4 strip sets.
Cut 48 segments.

4. Stitch 2 segments together as shown to make a four-patch unit. Press the seam in one direction. Make 24.

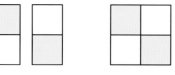

Make 24.

5. Stitch 1 blue 5½" x 5½" center square, 4 quarter-square-triangle units, and 4 four-patch units into 3 horizontal rows as shown. Press the seams in the direction shown. Stitch the rows together. Press the seams in one direction. Make 6 Star blocks.

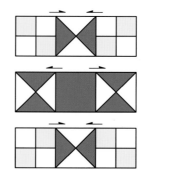
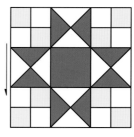

Make 6.

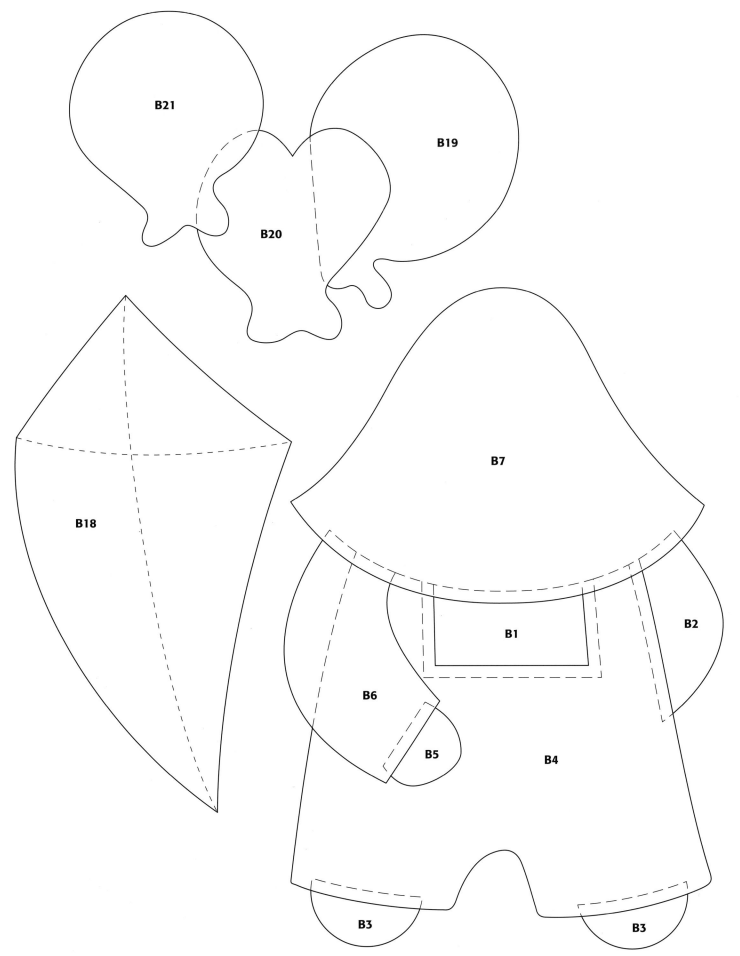

the appliquéd objects. Stemstitch the marked line. While the needle is still threaded with the embroidery floss, stitch the button to the end of the wagon pull string, leaving a thread tail on the top of the quilt at the beginning and end. Tie the thread tails in a knot; trim the ends to a uniform length.

4. Using the fine-tip black marker, refer to the patterns to mark the lines on the kites and the faces on the teddy bear and doll. Fill in the teddy bear's nose with the red marker. To make the doll's hair, thread the needle with 6 strands of the desired color embroidery floss; do not knot the end. Referring to the doll appliqué

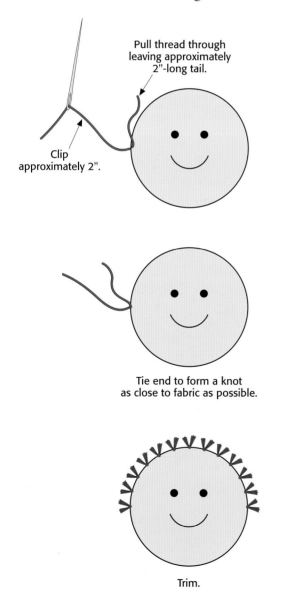

Pull thread through leaving approximately 2"-long tail.

Clip approximately 2".

Tie end to form a knot as close to fabric as possible.

Trim.

pattern, pull the floss from the front to the back of the quilt top where marked with an X, leaving a 2" tail on the quilt-top front. Bring the needle back up to the quilt-top front, slightly away from the first point of insertion; cut the thread 2" from the quilt-top front. Tie the 2 ends in a knot. Trim the ends ¼" from the knot. Repeat for the remaining Xs.

To make the kite tails, cut two 6-strand lengths of floss the color and length desired. Using 1 strand of matching embroidery floss, loosely tack a 6-strand length to the bottom point of each kite. Cut the ribbon into 2"-long pieces. Tie 4 to 5 ribbon pieces around the kite tail. Trim the ribbon ends to a uniform length.

5. Layer the quilt top with batting and backing; baste.

6. Quilt as desired.

7. Bind the quilt edges with the blue binding strips.

8. Stitch a label to the quilt back.

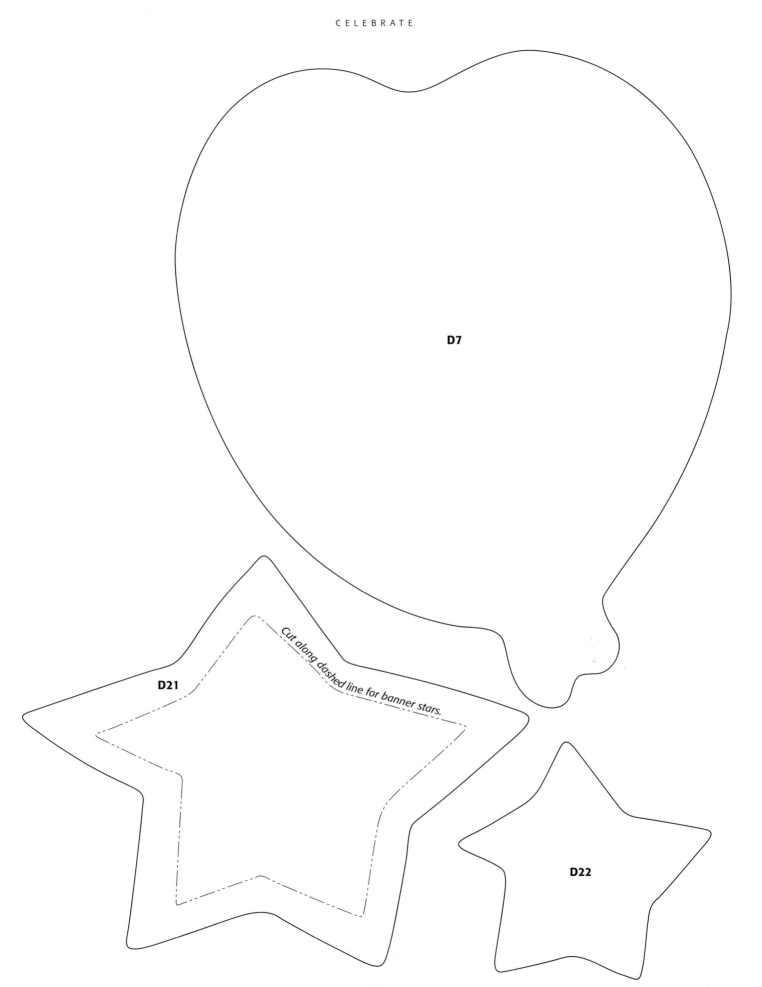

D7

D21

Cut along dashed line for banner stars.

D22

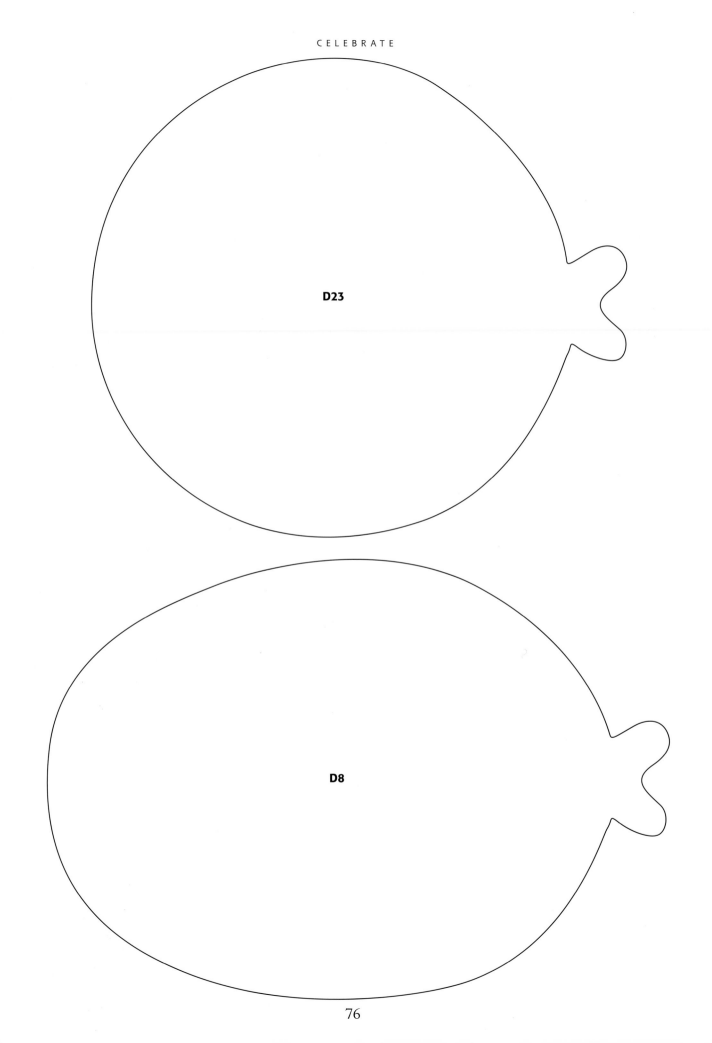

D23

D8

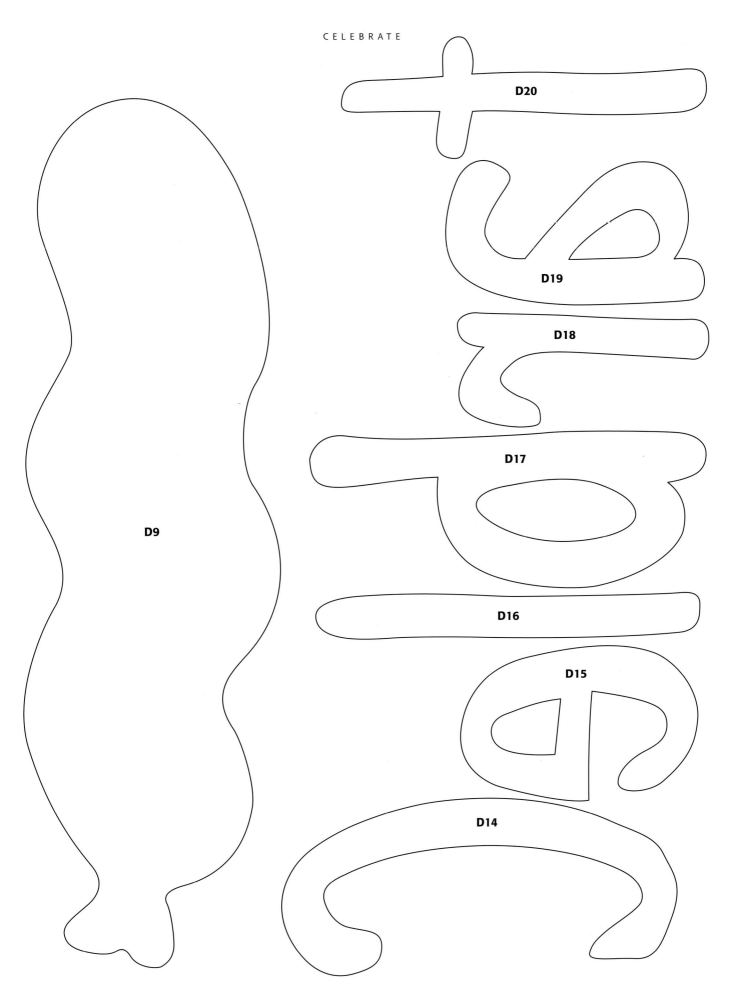

D20

D19

D18

D17

D16

D15

D14

D9

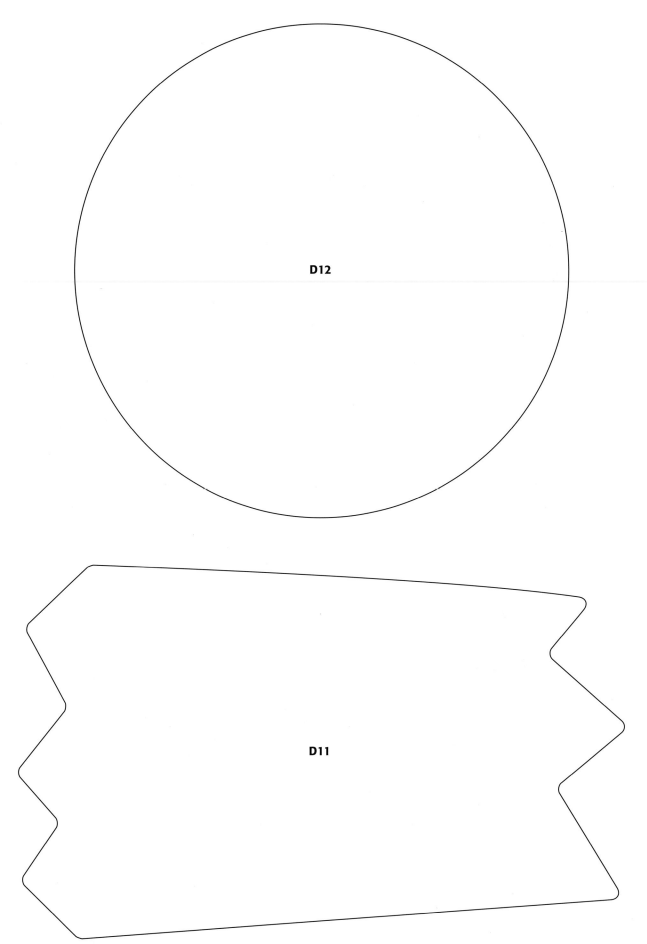

D12

D11

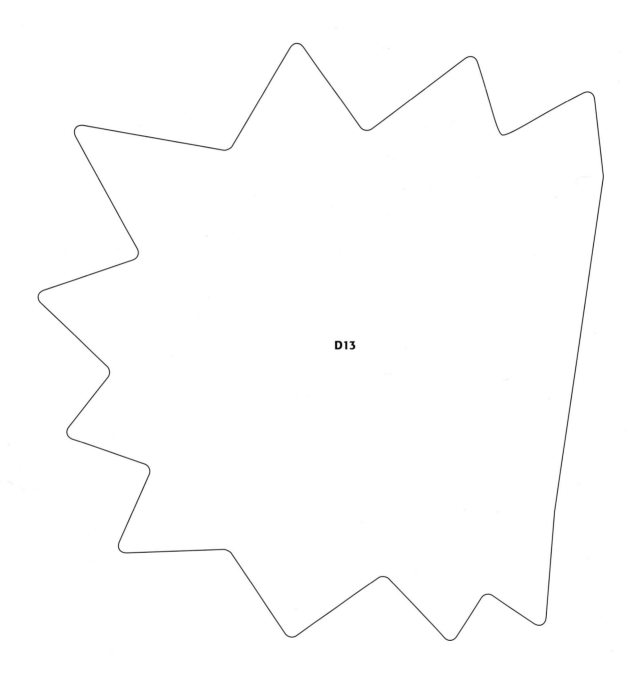

D13

About the Author

Photography by Peevyhouse

MARY M. COVEY is a quilter whose favorite part of the quilt process is design. She has been quilting for twenty years and has been teaching for at least fifteen of those years. Several of her designs have been published in both *Quilting Today* and *Miniature Quilts* magazines, and she has won numerous awards for her miniature quilts. In 1998 she began her own quilt-pattern company called the Good Life. Mary's book *A Snowman's Family Album Quilt* was published by Martingale & Company in 2000.

When asked how she began designing and quilting, Mary replied, "As a child I was always volunteering to help people do things. On more than one occasion this got me into a jam. When I was twelve, I volunteered to make my own costume for the children's play at church. There was only one problem. I did not know how to sew. My mother, however, gave me some pieces of fabric and showed me how to thread her machine. I remember lying on some newspaper and having my sister trace around my body to make a pattern. I cut and sewed and sewed and cut. Two days later I had created the ugliest, most wonderful costume ever. From that day on, I was hooked on designing and sewing.

"In the early '80s, I learned to quilt and rekindled that love for designing and sewing. I've been teaching quilting for fifteen years at the same shop where I first learned to quilt—the Cotton Patch Quilt Shop."

Mary is a member of the Green Country Quilt Guild as well as the Itty Bitty Quilt Committee, a stitch group devoted to miniature and small quilts. She lives with her husband, John, in Jenks, a small town just outside of Tulsa, Oklahoma. She has a daughter, Kristi, a son, Michael, and a daughter-in-law, Kristy.